MW00987312

WALK A LITTLE SLOWER

TANNER OLSON

WALK A LITTLE SLOWER

TANNER   OLSON

Walk A Little Slower: A Collection of Poems and Other Words
By Tanner Olson
writtentospeak.com

ISBN: 978-0-578-98342-4

Art direction & Interior Design: James Saleska / jamessaleska.com

Cover & Interior Illustrations: Tim Bauer / timbauerdesign.com

Editor: Andrew Milam

This book goes great with coffee.

i wrote this for you

just happy to be here

SLOW DOWN

LEAN IN

BEFORE YOU BEGIN...

Some of these poems were written to be heard.
Some of these poems were written to be read.
But all of these poems were written for you.

Slow down.
Sit with these words.
Give them time.
Stay awhile.

I think there is something in this book for you.

SLOW DOWN
LEAN IN
HOLD FAST
KEEP GOING

SLOW DOWN

I was eight years old the first time my grandma told me to slow down. My brother and I were thirty-five minutes away from the comforts of our bunk bed, bicycles, and parents, spending a weekend with grandma and grandpa in DeLand, Florida.

I can't remember why we were there, but that's where we were.

When you're eight, it is your job to go with the flow, to say please and thank you, and when you're feeling brave, to eat the vegetables the adults put on your plate without putting up a fight.

On our first day with our grandparents, they took us to KFC for dinner.
It was 4:00 in the afternoon, but we were told this was dinner, not a snack.

As a kid, I believed KFC was what kings and queens ate at their banquet tables.
I can't remember who suggested we go there to eat, but it was probably me.
I've always had a sophisticated palate.
My brother would eat whatever you put in front of him.
I was always the difficult child, a picky eater, only wanting what can be best described as "fair food."
To this day, fried chicken tops my list of favorite foods.
Followed closely by biscuits and mashed potatoes.
All of which are served at Kentucky Fried Chicken.
When it came to food, Colonel Sanders knew what he was doing.
And when it came to my health, I had no regard.

The inviting scent of fried chicken wrapped its arms around us as we walked through the doorway.
A bell rang as we entered the restaurant, almost to announce we had made the correct decision.
I stopped and looked around as if I had just entered a sacred space.
Perhaps we had.

Our grandpa told us we could get whatever we would like.
Challenge accepted, I thought.
The menu had poorly lit photos of each item, but I didn't mind.
I studied the menu more closely than I studied for any school test.
As I ordered, I pointed to photo after photo, remembering to say
please and thank you, purposely leaving off the vegetables.
Unless you consider mashed potatoes a vegetable.
If so, then half of my plate would be designated for vegetables.

Moments later, I was handed a full plate with the lingering words,
"You got it?"
I couldn't tell if the concerned look on the employee's face was due
to how much food I ordered or if I would be able to safely take my
plate from one end of the establishment to the other.

There was no way my soon-to-be greasy hands and salivating
mouth were going to let this plate of precious goods drop
to the floor.

I carefully navigated my way between empty tables to the highly
coveted corner booth.

Since it was 4:00 in the afternoon, we had our pick of seats.

While the others ordered, I sat patiently, admiring what
laid before me.

Fried chicken.
Biscuits.
Mashed potatoes.

Was I a king?
No.
But also, yes.

I tried to wait, but the intoxicating scent put a spell on me, stealing
my self-control and leading me into a moment of weakness.

It started with a nibble of the crispy skin of a chicken leg. This
delicious bite led to me shoveling food into my mouth as if I hadn't
eaten in days.

Fried chicken. Mashed potatoes. Biscuits.

There wasn't a bad bite to be taken.

Crumbs fell from my lips to my already stained t-shirt.

My feet, unable to reach the floor, swung with joy.

You would think my jaw was battery operated as it opened and shut without any signs of stopping.

My torso bounced back and forth as I did a happy dance in my seat as the food on my plate quickly disappeared.

Before I knew it, the food vanished as if I was a magician.

I swallowed my last bite as my brother and grandparents stepped to the table with their plates.

To their surprise, I had already finished my meal.

"Tanner!" exclaimed my grandma as she approached the scene of the crime. "Where did your food go? We didn't even say grace!"

I wanted to tell her that I had been thanking God with every bite, but I didn't want to push it.

For the next 20 minutes, I watched in silence as the three of them slowly ate their dinner.

Grandma continued to lecture me about how eating fast wasn't good for me and how it was rude to eat before others had even gotten their food.

I felt two kinds of full: overfull and shameful.

Every few minutes she would mutter how I was going to feel sick.

She was right.

My stomach was beginning to turn as it worked overtime attempting to process the already processed food. Every now and again, my body would jerk as I'd weather the storm of another food induced burp.

Some kids like getting into trouble.

I didn't.

But I somehow always found myself making the wrong choice.

Across the table my brother snickered, laughing at another one of my poorly executed decisions. He always knew better than I did. If my brother was best known for something, it was for doing things correctly. I, on the other hand, was best known for my impulsive behavior.

Every few bites, he would announce how good his food was, mentioning how he was going to savor every bite as if it was his last.

He knew all the right things to say.

Our grandpa was a man of few words, but in this moment, even his silence felt judgemental.

I thought my scolding was over, but grandma continued to tell me time and time again that I needed to learn how to slow down.

"Slow down," she would say before gingerly lifting a fork to her mouth.

I know those two words were spoken with love and sincerity, but I couldn't help but feel guilty.

She went on to tell me life was not meant to be rushed through but enjoyed.

I've had those two words rolling around in my head ever since she spoke them to me again and again that afternoon in the back corner booth of an empty KFC.

There are days when I remember them, but more often than not, those two words are far from my mind.

Sometimes it is the truth that is the hardest to remember.

I've rushed through meals and moments.
I've dreamed of being older when I was young and younger as I grow old.
I've blown through celebrations, emotions, and conversations.

But those two words continue to remain.

Slow down.

The other day would have been grandma's 101st birthday.

In her honor, I listened and slowed down.

I woke up before the alarm sounded.

Crawled out of bed and walked a little slower to the kitchen.

I put the coffee on and watched through the window as the sun began to make its way above my head.

The light seeped through the cracks in the blinds, filling the house with hope.

I opened my Bible and read a Psalm or two.

I wondered how often grandma would do this.

Sit and be.
Wait and watch.
Rest and remember.

I made toast.
I waited until it was golden brown, just the way I wanted it before removing it from the toaster.
I spread butter across the top, adding a little more than I needed just like grandma would.

I took one bite at a time, savoring every crumb.

No longer was I swinging my 8-year-old feet at the corner booth of a KFC.

"Slow down," I whispered to myself.

Grandma was right.

Life was not meant to be rushed through, but enjoyed.

Just like a plate full of fried chicken, mashed potatoes, and biscuits.

WALK A LITTLE SLOWER

I think today I'll walk a little slower and breathe a little deeper.

I'll leave my phone face down, inside, and give my eyes a rest to see beauty beyond a screen.

I'll grab a light jacket so I can still feel the cold wind, hold your hand until it gets sweaty, and I'll let go, but I'll never let go.

I'll walk below and between shadows, cut through the field, cross the street when the cars clear.

Today I want to find myself beneath the limbs of the trees and later on below a few million stars.

Maybe we'll see a dog or bump into old friends or both.

I'm not counting steps or miles, but I'm just walking because for now…

I can.

And I don't know what the future holds, if my days left are long or short or, well, you get it.

Maybe grief is around the corner or a missed call on my face-down phone back inside.

Maybe there is good news in my inbox or a miracle waiting in the welcome of next month.

In the morning, I'll sit a little longer and drink a little deeper.

I'll watch the light make its way through the dark morning.

The light always finds a way.

And I'll remind myself life won't always look the way it does.

Change is coming, and it might even be here.

I'll remember the steps forward and the steps back that led me to where I am and before I begin to move these feet once again, I'll slowly breathe in grace and exhale peace, knowing that every piece of me is here to be.

And whatever may become, well, for now,

For now, I'll walk a little slower and breathe a little deeper.

Because right now, I'm alive.

And everything is okay.

It's not perfect, and that's okay.

And that's what I'm learning to tell myself these days.

Everything is okay.

It's not perfect, and that's okay.

A JOURNAL ENTRY FROM ARCADIA, MI

I write this from the front porch of my in-laws' house in Arcadia, Michigan.

A man just drove by on a lawnmower, scaring the squirrels up trees.

Jimmy Eat World plays through the window behind me, while I sit writing in the *New Found Glory* t-shirt I wore yesterday.

This morning, I woke up slowly, reminding myself I have nothing to do today.

But I wanted to write or reminisce or something.

I'm in a place that reminds me of what was and amazes me at what has become.

I'm no longer pulling petals off of flowers, wondering if she loves me or loves me not.

If she loves me or loves me not.

If she loves me or loves me not.

She loves me.

We made breakfast together this morning, a breath of fresh air after a year of tornadoes and hurricanes and late night thunderstorms.

A year ago, I drove my red pickup truck south from Nashville to Texas, a day when chaos sparked the growing of two to become a better one.

I felt the call deep within to leave and could not say no.

Nothing inside me would let me say no.

I wanted to say no, but I didn't say no.

I can't explain it.

She came with me.

Yesterday, I ate two peaches.

"They were delicious," like the plums in William Carlos Williams' poem, "This Is Just to Say."

If you can eat a peach without getting messy, you don't know how to eat a peach.

With each bite, the peach juice dripped down my arm, tangling itself within a forest of right arm hair.

But it was worth it.

Even if I was left with a sticky mess to clean up.

It was worth it.

And this mess we are cleaning up continues to be worth it.

What was and what has become.
Moving and peaches.
Writing and reminiscing.
Jimmy Eat World and *New Found Glory*.
Chaos and clean up.
Tennessee and Texas.

All for the two to become a better one.

YOU'RE IN IT ALL

The wind is turning from warm to cool, sweeping in to send summer away, and I pray it will stay for another day.

But in the wrestling and wonder of the change, I'll sit still to see You're in it all.

How beautiful it is to believe You're in it all.

Before the leaves turn from green to brown, I'll wander alone below the setting sun.

Stepping through shadows as I listen to the great silence and sounds of the world as I leave behind and wander ahead.

And I feel like I'm always leaving something or someone behind and wandering ahead.

Past the present, one foot in front of the other, and I believe I'm walking forward straight into sure and certain, fall and forgiveness, sleepless nights and memories of warm summer sunlight.

Time keeps moving.

And I'm starting to think I can't keep up.

And I'm trying to be right where I am.

I'm trying to unwrap the present and cherish it like a fleeting summer day.

And I'm trying to remember that through it all,
spring to fall, and the months and moments between,
You're in it all.

99 CENT MANGO

Every week I buy a 99 cent mango from the store and wait for it to become ripe enough to eat.

It tests my patience as I wait to taste it.

And patience - like time - can be cruel and straining.

And I'm growing tired of watching and waiting.

Patience is birthed from expectation as we endure for something greater to arrive.

For all I have come to know, I am beginning to see patience is confidence that is ready and willing to continue through the pain and unknown.

In patience, we are purified, slowed down to see with clear eyes as our selfishness and desperation is refocused, handing us perspective and understanding in return.

Our appreciation grows with our longing, like Christmas or following a losing sports team.

And it is in seasons of patience I watch God work.

There is magic in His movement and grace in His giving, and most days, I forget I'm living between the two.

Like, I forget patience isn't a painful punishment but the way to much more.

To something so sweet.

So delightful.

So rich.

Like a 99 cent mango.

COMPASSION

You didn't say anything.

You just sat there.

Next to me.

With me.

For me.

You didn't try to make it better.

You didn't begin to rationalize or minimize or socialize.

You just sat there.

Next to me.

With me.

For me.

And when I spoke, you listened.

You didn't offer advice or attempt to say something nice.

You didn't tell me how I was feeling or what I was needing.

You didn't interrupt or disrupt.

You just sat there.

Next to me.

With me.

For me.

And when I got quiet, you didn't try to fill the silence.

You didn't.

It's like you knew I didn't need you to say anything.

You just sat there.

Next to me.

With me.

For me.

And I let you know when I was ready to get up and go.

And you came with.

Next to me.

With me,

For me.

FALL IS COMING

The sun never sleeps in the summer, and I don't want to either.

The last thing I want to miss is the rising morning mist and the fireflies in the fields at night.

I want to catch every glimmer of light that rises and falls before fall finds us.

I want to run with my bare feet through the streets again.

Ride my bike while wearing wet swim shorts again.

Have a peanut butter and blackberry jam sandwich on the beach again.

Take a nap on my back in the green grass again.

Place my bet on who will win,
me or the sun,
after ordering a double-scoop of chocolate chip cookie dough in a waffle cone.

Ice cream is perfect but somehow tastes better in a waffle cone.

I know summer won't last forever and fall is coming - but it's not here yet.

And tonight, we'll press play on old summer nights.

Reliving the moments we can't get back, the moments we desperately want to get back.

And tonight you'll find us around the fire while we sit with whiskey to sip as we have a serious summer talk about what was and what could be and how we used to eat peanut butter and blackberry jam sandwiches below the sun.

Old friends talking about what only old friends could know.

And it is good to be known.

PHONE

I didn't look at my phone yesterday.

Perhaps I could have survived the Oregon Trail or the 1970s or that camping trip I said no to three weeks ago.

Two days ago, without thinking, I felt my hands reach
for my phone.

It was a reaction.

If you asked my hands why they did this, they would say, "This is just what we do."

My fingers are addicted to holding something with such
great power.

My eyes are drawn by the light like a bug with a death wish.

My heart needs to be broken at least three times a day, just as my spirit needs to be crushed.

But yesterday I said no.

I left my phone plugged in on the other side

of my bedroom.

My mother always said, "Out of sight, out of mind."

She was talking about cookies.

But I think it applies to my phone.

Have you ever felt naked and proud?

I haven't.

But yesterday I did.

Without my phone, I felt free.

I felt myself coming back into my body.

I heard my soul whisper, "Isn't this better?"

And I think it is.

ONE OF THESE DAYS

One of these days you'll see.

You'll see it's always been worth the fight.

You'll see it's always been worth the love.

You'll see it's always been worth the reach.

You'll see it's always been worth this and much more.

You'll see He was always with you.

You'll see hope was alive the entire time.

You'll see darkness run from the light.

You'll see there was more happening.

There was more happening.

One of these days you'll see.

One of these days you'll see.

You'll see.

COFFEE

I've got stained teeth and burnt breath but a beat that's staying alive in my chest.

I've been waking up early to sit with the sunrise and watch Your beauty meet my barely open eyes.

The light breaks through, reminding me I can make it through.

And it's the first morning sip that reminds me of grace and what I can only imagine is a smile on Your face.

And for a moment, it's just You and me and a cup of coffee watching the waking world beginning to be.

The other morning I read, "Blessed are those who have not seen and yet have believed," and I am beginning to see I do not need to see You to believe You are with me.

You are.

You are with me.

And it's almost as if every sip brings us together.

And if that brings us together, we'll never be apart.

BLOOMING

I wonder what is happening that I cannot see. Something below the surface or beyond the horizon or between the questions and answers. A spark, a whisper, a prayer. And today I don't need to know what, I just want to trust that something more is happening. To let go and remember the beauty of becoming, the joy of blooming. Trusting that small faithful steps lead us further than we could ever dream or imagine. And I imagine I'll continue to dream about what is happening that I cannot yet see. A hope, a moment, a breakthrough.

I NEED TO HEAR

When the quiet comes and fails to calm, there are things I
need to hear.

I need to hear everything is going to be okay.

And I know I heard you tell me yesterday, but tell me again that
the way things are isn't the way they'll always be.

And I need to hear that it is love that casts out fear.

And I need to hear this is Christ's body and this is Christ's blood,
one was broken and one was poured, but both are for us.

And I need to hear about how grace is enough.

And I need to hear that we are still friends and that this is
not the end.

And I need to hear that this is not forever.

And I need you to help me remember.

And I need to hear from you because this life is too short
to not speak.

And this life is too hard to do alone week after week.

And this life is too much to go through without one another.

And this life is better when we hear from each other.

And I need to hear what it is you need to hear so when the
silence gets loud and quiet fails to calm, I can remind you that
everything is okay.

Everything is okay.

SILK & MILK

I had no idea what I was doing when I stumbled upon freedom as I let the words hit the page.

It was 7th grade when I felt the "feels" fall all over me.
My problems were pimples and puberty.
And I struggled to get my hair to sit the right way, and this was back when I used Axe body spray.
I had three armpit hairs, and my pants read Husky.

And in the confusion and voice cracking is when I first discovered the world of poetry.

And the first poem I ever wrote rhymed

silk with *milk*.

I wrote it in a college ruled spiral notebook, ripped it out along with the fringe, crumpled it into a ball and yelled, "*Kobe!*" as I launched a fadeaway to the corner trash can in our middle school language arts class, and that is how all of this began.

I discovered a brand new world of ink and imagination, emotions and endless fascination.

It was like God had taken off the training wheels and let me ride through the wind and rain, flying through the streets, passing surprises and shadows until the sun rose.

Baptized by the beauty, and now I believe I am what I always wanted to be: alive.

Alive by the glory of His grace and for peace,
this pen has taken these feet far, far beyond where I ever thought they could be, all because I started writing with wonder and questions and a chewed-up pen spilling faded black ink.

Through the flying high and feeling behind, through the constant comparison and attempts to change who I believe I was born to be, I found the secret hidden right in front of me:

None of us know what we are doing.

But we were made to be alive, to spread hope in this mixed up life, and here we are alive.

And I'm alive to be and I write to speak, live to seek, share to announce love and peace.

And this life of wondering and writing began in 7th grade when a teenage crush led these words to hit the page:

My heart is a flutter
As my words trip and stutter
All because
Her hair is like silk
The color of chocolate milk

PATIENCE

By now, the sun isn't far from climbing over the horizon. I know this because of yesterday and the day before and the day before…

Soon the darkness will be pushed to the other side of the world where they are beginning to say goodbye to today. And soon, just like yesterday, my shadow will move my eyes to the sky to see the beauty of the sunlight.

The cold of night will be replaced with the warmth of a new day, reminiscent of the words, "I forgive you."

And today, I'll give yesterday to the past
and let this be the present.

Whatever today brings,
whether silence or noise,
hopes or fears,
celebrations or tears,
I'll be here.

And soon the moon will arrive, bringing back the darkness and removing the light.

Just like yesterday and the day before and the day before…
But for now, light is on the way.

Light is always on the way.

STAY

Today all I can say is stay.

Stay.

And I know that may not be easy to hear, and this one word might bring fear, but stay.

Stay for the sunsets and sunrises and surprises that do somersaults straight into your soul.

Stay for the sequels and prequels because you never know if *Space Jam 2* will be a bust or beautiful.
Stay for the reunions and weddings and re-runs of *King of Queens* and *Freaks and Geeks*.
Stay for viral videos of animals doing what we thought they could only do in our dreams.

Stay to take another step with grace.
Stay to wake up to another day that could be the best day.

Stay to shake the slumber of your sleeping self.

Stay for confetti cake because confetti cake is good.

Stay for summer days at the lake and for the moments of give and take.

Stay.

And I know.

I know, today is hard.

And tomorrow might be too.
But move closer to see the beauty found within all that has come to be.
Let the light shine through all the cracks, scars, and questions and stay.

Stay.

And I know there are days when the last thing you want to do is stay, but if you stay for today then I'll see you tomorrow.

And tomorrow is worth staying for.

And maybe tomorrow we can have some confetti cake.

SONG I SANG

I remember old Wisconsin roads with brush off to the side.
I stepped over every broken crack because part of me still believed
the 2nd grade rhyme that it might break my mother's back.
Green pines stretched high above, branches intertwined, like
nervous first date hands.

And below, I walked alone through shadows and sunlight, hope
and heartbreak, up and down mountains of memories as I
thought of you.

Back when the song I sang sounded different then it does today.
Something changed when I left my life of alone for the
great unknown.

A holy transformation, a sacred becoming, knowing I had to stop,
surrender, and leave, to see the beauty found in the song my life
was learning to sing.

Stop, surrender, and leave.

To see my memories mix with the melody, thoughts coming
through with the rising tune, to finally rest in the resolution, and
that's when I returned to you.

It was always you.

A calm chorus sang, "We're gonna be okay."

I found harmony by your side.
A slow silence, an unforced rhythm coming forward toward the
honest promise of forever.

When I stopped is when I finally found the secret in the stillness,
the answer in the silence,
and a forever in the present.

And it is in your presence I sing a calm chorus,
"We're gonna be okay."

It was always you.

REMEMBER AND REST

And again I'll breathe in deep and exhale all that is heavy as I remember Your grace and mercy.

I'll lay down what's aching within as I lie down inside.

If my hope rests in You, so will I.

Lead my wandering mind to sit with the silence and remember all You've done as I wait for You to arrive.

Teach me to hold on and lean in and stay hopeful when I think of where and who I have been.

Unfold these white knuckled fingers and bring these hands to hand over what is keeping me from being still.

Restore to me the beauty of child-like believing, like before I heard about disease and death and before the war in my heart and mind started to steal my breath.

Push back my shoulders and set me straight as I pause in a world of constant motion.

Won't You remove what remains pressed on my chest so I can simply wait and rest?

And again, I'll breathe in deep and exhale all that is heavy as I remember Your grace and mercy.

And again, I'll breathe in deep.

And again, I'll exhale all that is heavy.

And again, I'll remember Your grace and mercy.

SLOW DOWN
LEAN IN
HOLD FAST
KEEP GOING

LEAN IN

"Lean into it," he said.

This isn't what I wanted to hear.

I wanted the easy way out.

I wanted him to tell me I needed to do nothing and that everything was going to work out.

But he didn't.

And he wouldn't.

He knew I needed to do the thing I didn't want to do.

And somewhere deep within, I knew I needed to do the thing I didn't want to do.

This wasn't the first time Trevor has told me something I didn't want to hear.

While in college, he called me out for my desire to be loved and accepted by all.

He told me I had compromised who I was

in order to be liked by whoever stood in front of me.

He saw right through the person I presented.

He told me I could just be me.

I could just be me.

It was something I didn't know I needed to hear, but I did.

It was as if he was the only one who saw the mask I had on.

Freedom can be found in the faithful words of a trusted friend.

Trevor is that.

We've been close since we first met at 19. Complete opposites knitted together by a love for God and His Kingdom. Together we've confessed sins, celebrated the Lord's Supper, traveled the country, and stood by each other on our best days and our worst days.

I wouldn't be the person I have become if it wasn't for Trevor.

But when he told me to lean into it, I didn't want to admit he was right.

But he was right.

So I did.

I had the conversation I didn't want to have.

And it hurt.

But it was the right thing to do.

I've always been better at running from hard things, rather than leaning in and taking the next right step.

I've been trying to take Trevor's advice and apply it to other areas of my life.

To lean in.

More and more, I am reminding myself to lean in to the truth.

It's often difficult and uncomfortable, and it often means I have to be vulnerable and honest.

The promises I so easily forget are the ones I need to be leaning into.

Many times, I have forgotten forgiveness, misplaced peace, taken my eyes off of grace, and let His sovereignty slip my mind.

But when I turn to Scripture, I see so clearly that God is always inviting us to lean into what He has for us.

And what He has for us is far better than anything we could ever imagine.

Or so I am beginning to believe.

Lean in.

See what happens.

See what changes.

Because something certainly will.

LIFE IS MESSY

Life is messy, but so is art.

Both a process, often never finished, left undone with more to be done or re-done.

Hands dressed up from thumb to wrist with dried up paint chips cracking from creating.

Below my feet lies the wasteland of waste, crumpled papers with crooked lines and failed designs, like 2009 and lump-in-the-throat confessions beginning with, "That one time."

Life is messy, but it's beautiful.

It is the ink we spill and the hues we blend that depicts a story of something more.

And it's unfolding before our eyes, changing as the brush strokes and sun rises and falls, and it is beautiful.

Out of sight the roots sink to dive deep, a shifting of the dirt below making their way like we make ours, like the drying of watercolors or the fading of chalk on a sidewalk, a give and take.

Roll over to wake, live to write memories on a journal page that connect and divide catching the eye like the sculpture behind the glass.

Mirroring more than can be ignored, a glance to gain a glimmer of hope.

Sharpened pencils and faded erasers are testimonies to the stories we write and the art we live like breathing and believing it's all life-giving like a simple seed or idea that has come to be.

And it's beautiful.

Hung or framed or displayed only to be found in, with, and under God's grace, like a celebration of freedom in the middle of a raging storm or gallery or Friday night or the heavy or the light.

Never finished, only begun.

And it's beautiful.

Each breath is another stroke across the canvas, a scribble of life found within the madness and the questions and the waking to another day only to see this work in progress is becoming.

And all of this, it is beautiful.

Fragile and imperfect.

Outside the lines, free from perfect rhyme.

Messy, but beautiful.

All of this, it is beautiful.

REMEMBER

I had skinned knees and a red tank-top, a child's matching outfit, missing front teeth, but I had everything I would ever need.

I remember Saturdays, 33 minutes away, Raymond Avenue and Papa's blue pickup truck. Shoulder to shoulder and side by side with my cousins and brother as we rode in the bed beneath the clear Florida sky, next to orange groves and pineapple trees that were more like bushes, we found corners of the forest that had never been touched.

We filled our fingernails with dirt as we dug for buried treasure, chased after snakes before I knew I was afraid of them, innocent hands swinging plastic swords and firing water guns to defend the land our grandfather built with his bare hands.

We were given backyard hose baths after we finished our popsicles, clearing away the sticky streaks of red and blue that raced down our forearms. Car keys began to appear as rumblings of "Goodbye!" and "It was so good to see you!" filled the family room.

The sun stepped away, pulling its light through the leaves and Spanish moss of the giant oak trees and the thick clouds of cigarette smoke that poured from the mouths that said, "I love you."

To this day, I love that smell of cigarette smoke like I love what life once was.

CAKE FOR BREAKFAST

I ate the leftover cake from your birthday for breakfast.

I had to.
I was sad.
I know, it wasn't the right choice, but it also wasn't the wrong one.
Also, it's Monday.
Again.
They never seem to stop arriving.
And that's a good thing - or so I am trying to believe.

Halfway through the morning, I found frosting on the outside of my hand, the same place where I would find smudges of green crayola marker as I'd scribble the grass in my 2nd grade class.

Back when I looked forward to Mondays.

And back when I could have cake for breakfast.
Well, a muffin.
But we all know muffins are just morning cake.

Before school, I'd have an Otis Spunkmeyer Chocolate Chocolate Muffin for breakfast because I didn't like eggs or oatmeal.
Something about texture.
And I really just wanted cake for breakfast.

I mean, a muffin.

And today, just like when I was 7, I needed to begin my day with something sweet so I could move my feet.

Because sometimes you just need to have cake for breakfast.

WHAT I'LL DO TODAY

Mary Oliver once asked,
What do you plan to do with your one wild and precious life?

And I don't know.
I don't know what I'll do with my one wild and precious life, but today I'll enjoy being alive.
I'll open the window and feel the wind blow through.
I'll turn off my phone and find peace in the unknown.
I'll thank God for grace and linger a little longer after she kisses my face.
During the day, I'll sit beneath the glow of the sunshine, and at night, I'll pour a little more wine.
I'll even write a few lines that don't rhyme.
Today, I'll be my full self.

I'll be me.
Today, I can only be me.
And today, like Jim Valvano once said, *"There are three things everyone should do every day...*
Laugh...
Think...
And have your emotions move you to tears."
And that's what I'll do today.
That's what I'll do with my one wild and precious life.

A DIFFERENT KIND OF AMAZING GRACE

The sun slept in this morning,

leaving the rain to wake the day.

Pitter patter alarm splashing silence,

a different kind of amazing grace.

My legs stretched sore from yesterday's Friday, weak from carrying a week's worth of weight.

Veins coursing with leftover hope from Thursday, reheated from the meal on Sunday

and someday,

Someday, I'll close my eyes and see it all too clearly.

Wednesday welled up weaknesses, a dry river of lost love, the mess I've made, the list of wrongs continues to grow long.

A sour aftertaste of Tuesday's thoughts

Monday managed to keep in mind.

If it wasn't for Sunday, I'd never have made it to Saturday.

A refreshed soul, ready to begin tomorrow again.

LET IT SHINE

We used to sing, "This little light of mine," and I've been trying to "let it shine, let it shine, let it shine," but the shine has been scorched by storms.

Wind and waves wrecked my way, and I'm looking to be restored.

To breathe with ease, to walk in peace, and to sing of a love I knew before.

There is a piece of me that is lost in the future and stuck in the past, but I've been trying to slow down and remember the words that continue to last:

Come to me all who are weary.

Because I've been needing some rest.

To unplug and confess;
To sit and be and thank You for all that has come to be,
To remember the love I knew before, before the world broke and bent my knees to the floor.

And I'm beginning to see that
where You are is where there is hope.
And slowly I am coming to know,
You won't let me go.

You won't let me go.

And that light, even in the storms and night and when things feel far from right, that light, continues to shine bright.

A POEM ABOUT THE THINGS I LOVE

I love poems that begin the same way they end.

I love full circles, like returning to where I began, and seeing the leaves turn from green, to brown, to ground, to green again.

And I love basketball, the feel of the ball, the sound of squeaking shoes, but what I love most is how it reminds me of my dad.

How after mowing the lawn, we would shoot hoops in the street below the Florida sun, just father and son.

I love the smell of rain and the haunting sight of dark clouds.

I love déjà vu.

I love déjà vu.

And I love food that makes me hurt.

If you listen carefully you can hear the bells of Taco Bell ringing and my stomach is ready to start singing.

I love feeling home in an empty room, and I love when you text me, and I wish you'd do it more.

I love when the windows are down and the music is loud.

I love black coffee.

Ethiopian pour over, if you will, but diner coffee will always taste like Saturday mornings at The Town House as we'd watch the chickens cross the road.

I love dogs and most days, I wish I was one.

I love words and how they can move us and heal us and shake us and shift us and leave us different.

I love front porches and rocking chairs and rocking with you without being distracted by our phones.

And I love romantic comedies, and I don't know why, and I don't care if you don't, but do you remember in *How to Lose A Guy In 10 Days* when we knew what was going to happen but didn't know how?

I liked that.

I don't know why, but I did.

I love couches that hold you like a baby.

And it goes without saying because I'm a breathing human being, but I love chips and queso.

I love road trips and carpet and spicy chicken sandwiches from Chick-fil-A, and that's all I have to say.

Except, I love when we are together.

The heavy loneliness melts away, and you're the light that welcomes me home to stay.

The hands that wrap warmth around; the look in your eyes is a gift that keeps this list long.

And for a moment, I'm no longer stressed out or bummed out, I'm just happy to be here.

I'm just happy to be here.

With you, I'm just happy to be here.

I love poems that begin the same way they end.

AND WE CAN STILL

A poem written during the Coronavirus Pandemic

and we can still dance
and bake brownies
and we can still wave as we pass
and text about it later

we can still stay up late and chase dreams

we can still put off doing laundry and leave the dirty
dishes in the sink

and we can still rewatch The Office
and cringe during Scott's Tots

and we can still pour coffee in the morning
and again in the afternoon
and we can still take hot showers
and plant gardens with bright colorful flowers

and we can still look for the good
and keep going even when we feel misunderstood

and we can still live without our phones
and find joy in being alone

and we can still read books on the couch at home
and maybe even write our own
and we can still order take out and write letters
and we can still chase the sunset
and scream in the rain to ease the pain

and we can still believe
and breathe
and isn't that a beautiful thing

and we can still open our hands to pray
and empty our lungs as we sing
and we can still move forward

we can still build a better tomorrow today
because we still have today
we still have today
we only have today

YOU AND I

and i read about how he kneeled with the lost

and sunk to the lonely

and sat with the outcast

and different

and i see how He loves

and how He leads with love

and not hate

and how when He bled it was not for the red white

and blue but for

you and i

and how He rose for all and not just the right or left or them
or us but all

and i'll stop and pray on bent

and sore knees for those who have been cut

and kicked and cursed to their own

and i'll weep with those who weep

and i'll sink

and sit with those shaking in fear

and i'll rise

and speak for those who are silent

and i may never comprehend the depth of fire-fueled hate or
endure knife-cutting slurs but i'll stand

and remain hand-in-hand with those who are brave
enough to remain

and stand

and i'll pray for the hurting and hated

and even though it hurts to say i will pray for those who hurt and hate

and tell us we shouldn't and they shouldn't stay

and i'll pray for the enemies of love

and friends of bigotry

and i'll pray they see love has a place

and may they meet love face to face

and turn from wicked ways towards glorious grace

and i'll sing a song of praise knowing Christ came

and He will come again

and this is not the end

and this is not the end

and this is not the end

and when i say amen, i will rest in peace

and may this peace go beyond me

and stretch to you

and bring others to see the truth

and may we stretch together

and stand together

You and i

not us and them

but

You and i.

THE HOPE OF FOREVER (1000 STRONG)

I'm only here for a minute, and I want to make it count before time runs out.

While I'm here, I want to be present.

Available and able to avail, to live with palms face up among closed fists,
to spread hope in a world where it is hard to exist.

I'm not here to prove I am right but to love the person to my left and right.

To do the small things that matter with humility and sincerity.

Like inviting people to the table.

To come forward toward a forever.

To connect to the depth of what it means to be forgiven and free.

Standing to see that all of this is from and for all of You.

And when Jesus said, "Follow me," He never said it would be easy.

But He also never sent us alone.

And I know in all of this, I am not alone.

We go together.

Can you hear the sound of steps multiplying?

A thousand strong to continue moving the hope of forever along.

I'm only here for a minute, and I want to make it count.

THIS & THAT

Life is full of this and that, and I'm learning to balance what was, what is, and what could be.

How to be present and process the past while looking to the future.

And my prayers rise and fall in my head and out of my mouth with faith and sometimes fear, but I know through it all, He hears when I am loud and when I am clear.

Lately I've been up early to rise, to meet the morning right after night, to open my eyes as soon as they shut tight.

It's been awhile, but I've started praying once again.

Will you show me when to
let go and hold fast?
Go first and be last?
Say yes and ask why?
Leave it behind and still try?
Give and receive?
Rejoice and grieve?
Inhale and exhale?
Sit with the silence and shout the truth I believe?

Between the start and the end,
will You teach me how
to continue to begin again
and again?

YOU ALONE

As we come before You with another day, won't You hear
us as we pray?
Before You we sit, before You we are.

And You,
You are before all things.
And all things work through You and for You and with You.

And all things are held together by You and You alone.
And when I am alone, help me to know I am seen and known.
And I am not alone.
That You see me.
And You know me.
And You love me.
And that is enough for me.

You bring light to the darkness and hope to the hopeless,
and sometimes I feel like I am somehow, someway caught
between the two.

But even in the in-between, You are there with me.

Lead my heart to wonder and wander
in the depths of where we are going,
of where You have already been, to walk with You through the
now and then.

And then, may I see with clear eyes that

through all of this and that,

through what was and what will be,

You have always been.

And You alone are enough for me.

I WANT TO WRITE SOMETHING

I want to write something that will move you beyond yourself.

To piece together the right amount of syllables in a style that will steal your anxiety and leave you hopeful.

To spill silhouettes of memories and truth that will bring you back to the days of your youth.

I want to write something that will shake you to your core and leave you wanting more.

Like the last line of *Harry Potter and the Deathly Hallows* or the center of a cinnamon roll or the voice of Morgan Freeman how it speaks to our heart and soul.

I want to write something that will make you laugh and then cry and then laugh again and leave you thinking maybe he's a comedian.

Like, Ray Romano.
Except, not as nasally.

I want to write something where I don't talk about Ray Romano or how we used to watch *Everybody Loves Raymond* as a family after we finished dinner.

I want to write something that will bring you back to your childhood. To the times when you would fall but get back up again, to when we would share our stories and compare our scars like the one I got when I crashed my bike into a parked car.

Back to the mornings where pancakes were the only option and calories, like salaries, were only things adults had to think about.

Back to the days when our hands didn't hold phones but held another hand.

Back to the nights when you would whisper, "Good night," to stuffed animals and we swore we heard them say, "Sleep tight."

Back to a time before the world kicked the weird out of you and me, and there was no such thing as normal.

Back to a time when after dinner you would watch *Everybody Loves Raymond* because it was on.

I want to write something that will put a pain in your side and maybe even a tear in your eye.

I want to write something that will make you look at the person you love like never before.

But sometimes, I want to write something that will make you think of your boyfriend and wonder, how come he isn't more like this guy?

I want to write something that will make you think that poetry isn't the worst.

I want to write something that will move you, change you, inspire you and make you forget that you have the internet in your pocket.

I want to write something that makes you feel seen and known, words that will sit with you when you feel alone.

I want to write something that will pull you away from what's keeping you from being here.

I want to write something that will make your emotions nod their head and maybe even something that will make your foot tap, fingers snap, hands clap, something that will make you get your phones out and say, "You gotta check this guy out," in your group chat.

Or something like that.

I want to write something that will help you remember God and grace and how you aren't the only one who feels like you're all over the place.

I want to write something and I know this is something, but is this anything?

Is this anything?

I want to write something, but right now, this is all I have.

CONFESSION

I know You know everything, but I can't hold onto what's breaking within.

My hands hold regrets, and my mind continues to replay the pain I've caused.

I confess that I have been a mess.

Forgive me, for I have been far from who You created me to be.

It is with my thoughts and my words and my actions that I have misrepresented grace, and I have turned my back on love.

Wash me white.
Let it be love that brings me through this night.

Through it all, the walk and the fall,
Have mercy on me.
Forgive me.

Change me.
Lead me.

I'll keep close the peace You promise and leave far behind the fear You called us from.

Help me let go of what's keeping me from You.

Help me let You take away what's keeping me from You.

Have mercy on me.
Forgive me.

Change me.
Lead me.

GATHER TOGETHER

Gather together like the thunder and rain clapping and colliding in the sky, like the waves and wind rushing straight to the sea's shore.

Gather together.
Where truth is louder than the lies and where friends and family remind each other of the truth as they text what should be yelled.

Gather together.
Beneath the oak tree in a field where the golden hour finds you as if it was invited to join.

Gather together.
Let the daylight remind you summer is bringing a new season and a sunset and change.

And let the change remind you we were made to.

To change and to gather together.

THROUGH TODAY AND INTO TOMORROW

Let it be faith that moves me forward.

Let it be hope that heals.

Let it be peace that passes through all my pain.

Let it be mercy that meets me in the morning.

Let it be joy I leave behind.

Let it be love that leads me through today and into tomorrow.

SILENCE

Right now, God, I don't have the words.

I don't know what to say, but I know there is much more that is
said in my silence.
And sometimes, it's the silence that reminds me of the certainty.
It's the pain that points to the promise.
And it's the night that leads me to the morning light.

In all that is uncertain, I am certain You are for me through every
little thing.

Faithfulness doesn't always make a noise.
It is the quiet that keeps me close to You.

Hope doesn't always whisper or yell.
It is the moments of nothing that remind me You are everything.

In all that it is unknown, I know that I am known.
And when we are known, we are far from alone.
May my silence be faithful.
And when there are no words to be said,
I know You know what I am saying in my silent surrender.

CAMPHOR TREE

Out the back door of our childhood home grew a growing Camphor tree.

The sunshine crawled through the cracks in the bright green leaves, space created by the Southern breeze.

Below its wide canopy fell little black berries, but we were told to keep them out of our mouths like naughty words and dessert before dinner.

To my young eyes, the branches swayed like the fingers of giants, pointing east and west, and I did my best to climb their arms with my little limbs, pulling myself higher and higher before I was told to,

"Come on down."

And no matter how many times I close these eyes, I can't get back to the way it used to be when I was 8 and he was 9.

And I'm still trying to close my eyes to get back to the way it used to be, when I'd walk out the back door and find myself beneath the canopy of the growing camphor tree.

Now that I'm back inside, I've come to realize I was never prepared to say goodbye to my childhood or that growing camphor tree.

And I'm still trying to bring myself alive, to climb high, to hear my mom call me back inside and hear those three words,

"Come on down."

SLOW DOWN

LEAN IN

HOLD FAST

KEEP GOING

HOLD FAST

Leaves of green surrounded me as my fingers wrapped tight around the branch above. The sun made its way through the open spaces in the leaves, lighting my every move as I climbed higher. The blades of grass below began to get smaller as I made my way to the sky.
I was seven and smiling.
I was missing teeth, but had everything I needed.
I was fully alive.

Our neighborhood backed up to a busy road bridging two towns. From the branches of the camphor tree, I would watch the cars pass by, waving to the truck drivers, signaling for them to honk their loud horns. From time to time, they would, and even though I knew it was coming, I'd get startled, almost falling.
Our neighborhood wrapped around in a near perfect oval, a row of houses on the outside and a row on the inside.
On our block, it was as if *The Sandlot* met *The Mighty Ducks*.

A neighborhood full of young boys.
Bikes and ramps and skinned knees.
Swimming pools and Marco Polo and pruny hands and the echoes of boys yelling, "*Fish out of the water.*"

N64 parties and rumble packs and Cheeto-dust coated fingers and crushed cans of Coca-Cola.
Basketball in the road and football in the front yard and cops and robbers up and down our safe street.

Adventures from sun up to the flickering of street light posts, and on our luckiest nights, the waking of stars in the open southern sky.

But it was up in that camphor tree where I felt fully alive.

Above the ground, just below the clouds, there was nothing keeping me from being free.
There wasn't a to-do list in my pocket.
There wasn't a sin I was losing sleep over.
There wasn't the fear of the unknown lurking in my mind.

There wasn't a worry in the world.

I was young.
I was free.
I was free to dream.
I was free to rest.
I was free to become.

Most summer nights, as the stars began to peak their way through the black Florida sky, my mom would yell into the backyard, "Come on down!"

I didn't want to.

Dinner was ready, but I wasn't.
I never wanted to leave the freedom found within the branches of the camphor tree.
It had grown to become my sanctuary, my hiding place.

The camphor tree in our backyard was planted a few years after I was born. Our limbs grew free beneath the Florida sun as we stretched towards the sky together. Some kids around the neighborhood had tree houses and playsets with swings, but I had all I needed in this tree: freedom. Like Mowgli from *The Jungle Book*, I was wild and barefoot, home between the branches, an adventure above the ground.

"Come on down," rang in my ears as I gripped tight the branch above my head.
I let my bare feet slip from the branch, leaving my legs to dangle feet from the ground.

My fingers began to lose their grip as the bark dug into my worn skin.
I held tight and counted down from 10.

My feet hit the ground right after I exclaimed, "One!" and my back slowly slid down the trunk of the tree. I sat still beneath the canopy of the camphor tree before returning inside.
There wasn't anything wrong with what was waiting for me inside our house.

Parents who loved me, a brother who called me his friend, and a cat who sometimes let me pet her. But I needed to soak up one final moment of freedom before going inside.

I slowly ran my hands across the tops of the blades of grass.
It was soft and growing and full of life.
Just like my seven-year-old self.
I brushed my hands off and skipped my way to the door where my mom called from.

I didn't know it at the time, but this wasn't going to last forever.
Nothing seems to last forever.
Basketball in the street, N64 parties, jumping bikes off ramps.
It would eventually come to a close.

As children, parents and grandparents find ways to weave comments into conversations that would leave me to shrug my shoulders and go the other way.

Comments like, *"You don't know what you have until it's gone,"* and, *"Enjoy it while you can,"* and, *"You know, one day you won't be able to eat that."*

I didn't think so, but they were right.

They were always right.

It seems like a blink of an eye ago I was among the branches of the growing camphor tree.
My child-sized fingers wrapped around the bark as I dreamed about the future and now the present has found me dreaming about the past.

And most days, I want to be back in the branches of the growing camphor tree.
I want to wave to truck drivers and beg them to honk their horns.
I want my pockets and mind to be empty of to-do lists and worries.
I want to greet the stars as they make their nightly appearance.
I want to be seven and smiling again.
And I want to hear my mom call from inside, "Come on down!"

I'VE NEVER SEEN A MOOSE IN THE WILD

There are days when the thought of leaving slips into my mind. It's a thought that is dark and far from kind. And most of the time I wonder how it worked its way to a place that leaves me feeling burdened, blind, and behind. But I'm fine. At least that's what I tell myself from time to time. But I can't leave. I can't leave because I have yet to see the sun set over and through the redwood trees. And I can't leave because I have yet to find rest in the mess and I still have a little something more to give than my best. And I can't leave because next Saturday I made plans and I don't want to be late. And I can't leave because I love the way she cooks and part of me wonders at age 74 how I will look. And as silly as it sounds, I've never seen a moose in the wild. And I want to see a moose in the wild.

And I can't leave because for as hard as living can be I can't help but believe there is beauty beginning to bloom out of the brokenness. I believe there is. And I am going to see it.

I GUESS

And I guess I am still wondering about everything below and
above, about death and decay, about life and love.

And what it means to be a man and what it means to understand.

And some days, I wish I could wash away the constant wonder
and rest in the reverberating beauty of the love that keeps me from
going under.

To accept what is with both hands, but then I wonder if I should
or if I could and maybe I just want to be understood.

And I guess I'm a little bruised and a little broken.
I feel less like a blessing and more like a burden.
And I'm still not sure how to use that word,

blessing.

I guess I am a little scared to ask why,
a little fearful to try,
a little hesitant to open my eyes.

But still, I can't get away from the hope that it is You who is
standing by my side.

That it is You who is whispering deep into my wonder that I won't
sink or go under.

That it is You who is reminding me that all of this is going to
be alright.

All of this is going to be alright.

IT IS GOOD

Darkness takes its turn, and I'm ready for the light to return.

For the flowers to bloom and for the shine to come through.

Let the snow melt away and let joy make a way.

I'm still hoping for a better day.
And I'm still finding ways to play.
And I'm still making wishes on my birthday.

And I'm still yelling, "*Kobe*" as I fadeaway.
And I'm still believing when I pray.
And I'm still reminding myself it is going to be okay.

And I'm still coming back to the hope that led me through what was to what is.

And what has become is never what I thought it would be.

I never thought today would look this way and as hard as it is to say, it is good.

It is good.

and maybe this is what it means
to believe and be
and maybe this is what
it feels like for these
feet to have faith
and for these
hands to hold hope
and maybe this is what I need
to move forward
to keep moving forward
through all of this
and in all of this
even what remains misunderstood
I'm still saying
it is good
it is good

I READ YOUR POEM YESTERDAY

I read your poem yesterday.
Your words, like always, were beautiful.
And they still, like the last poem you sent, continue to ring
inside my mind.
I read the third line four times before moving on.
And I read your poem once more before I walked out the door this
morning as if it was my breakfast to go.
I'm still digesting them and that's what's so troubling.

I can't decide if I am reading them how they were written.
As I read them, I get to decide when to read the next word and
when to pause and when to begin again, and I wonder if that is
how it's meant to be heard.

And please don't tell me that this poem is a gift for me to have and
to have it however I'd like.

If that's the case, you can have these words back.

I want to hear you read your poem.
I want to hear you share what you sent.
I want to listen to where you pause and where you begin again.
And I want to see the look in your eyes skim the paper your hands
clutch close.
And I want to see if you tremble over stanza 6 or make it through
the last few lines because I can hardly make it through those
last few lines.

Read them so they can ring inside my head like they ring
inside yours.

HEADED EAST

I'm headed east beyond my wildest dreams with my loudest fear.

Through the twists and turns of Tennessee,
I began to see the beauty unfold in a moment of discovery.
Knoxville felt like home.
Spilled my heart and soul to a room full of strangers and a few good friends.

And that night, she prayed for doors to open.
For there to be a breakthrough; for these words to reach a few.
And she spoke the name *Father*, like she truly knew Him, and I think she truly knows Him.

I left town before the sun rose, pushed 75 as I looked around with the windows down.
I played some Tyson Motsenbocker as I made my way through the mountains as memories flashbacked.
I passed through Dolly Parton's hometown and sang, "Here You Come Again" as loud as I could again and again.

It's been quite some time since my feet felt North
Carolina's ground.
Asheville holds beauty and wonder, and I wanted her to be here with me.
My wife, not Dolly.
Well, both.

And it happened again.
That night as I stood in a puddle of the poems I poured out, she prayed over me before they sent me.
Their kindness was a gift, something I'll forever miss.

But like always, I had to go.

Virginia and Pennsylvania called and I answered.
A couple cups of coffee and a few hundred miles.

I drove through the fog and told my mom.
I called Kris, and we began to reminisce.
I talked to Taylor late into the night.

There is something about the comfort of a friend who helps you remember everything is going to be alright.

Through the snow and rain, I made my way straight into the dark of night because I wanted to be by her side.

I'll always drive through the night to make it home by tomorrow morning.

And I made it home.

Just in time to leave again.

But pretty soon I'll be singing, "Here You Come Again."

LET IT BE PEACE

Let it be peace that washes over me like the rising morning sun.

Place your hand on my back and slowly shake my soul awake.

Draw the curtains and bring my eyes to see there has always been beauty in front of me.

And there always will be.

Remind me again to take a deep breath and exhale and
one more time.

Fold open my hands and cleanse me of my sins like it's Sunday and
I'm shoulder to shoulder with other sinners confessing before we
taste the bread and drink the wine and hear the words,
"You're forgiven.
You're free.
Go in Peace."

And as I go, let this peace hold me like the arms of a mother and
guide me like the hand of a father.

Let this peace rewrite the past and shape the future and change
today to create a better tomorrow.

And tonight, when I close my eyes to fall asleep, let these hands
hand it all over, except for peace.

For peace is what I'll keep.

BE NOT AFRAID

Today I will live out those ancient words,
be not afraid.
I will be not afraid as fear begins to flood my mind and water rises
with my worry.
I will be not afraid as I think about the future and the questions
that begin to ring loud.
I will be not afraid as I lay down dreams that have slowly started
to die and I'm left holding one word, "Why?"
I will be not afraid as I plant seeds and water new dreams and pray
they come to life.
I will be not afraid of the enemy or his tricks or the night because I
know that joy comes with the morning light.

And it is always almost morning.

I will be not afraid of the unknown because I will continue to
remember that I am known.
And I will be not afraid as we continue to make our way through
all that is heavy, all that is here and all that is holy.
I will be not afraid for the Father has called me His.
I will be not afraid for Christ died only to rise, and He
will come again.
I will be not afraid for the Spirit lives within and moves me to
be not afraid.

I will hold tight to these three words, "Be not afraid," as they still
and forever hold true.

As they still and forever lead us beyond what we know to be true.

...HOLD ON

and on those days when nothing seems to be going right
...hold on.

and in those moments when life feels hopeless
...hold on.

and during those seasons of storms and uncertainty
...hold on.

and just like yesterday and the day before
I need to trust and breathe and
...hold on.

I JUST NEED TODAY TO BE EASY

I just need today to be easy.

For the rain to become sunshine.

For regrets to stay far from my heart and mind.

For the traffic to part and park
and for there to be more dogs than humans at the park.

And I need today to be a day where I do better than rhyme
park with park.

And maybe today I won't spill or get an unexpected bill.
And that pimple on my forehead will finally disappear.
And today when I think about the future, I won't begin to
sweat from fear.
And I don't need to see sirens in my rearview mirror.

Give me all the green lights and smiles from strangers, but not
creepy smiles, only smiles that remind me I can keep going.

And maybe today wars will cease
and you and I finally say, "Forgive me, please?"

And today, I won't over think or under think or forget to think,
but everything will be perfectly thought-out.

And you'll text me back right away so I don't get lost in the
wonder and wait.

And I'll remember it's okay for me to be this weight.

And today, I'll be on the couch by eight, unless we decide to
stay out late.

Like 9:30 late.

And today, I just need the internet to correctly connect.
And it would be nice to be shown some respect.

And maybe today a piece of bread won't leave me feeling completely wrecked.

And somehow, some way, nothing will chip or crash or crack.

And that ongoing pain won't come back.

And today will be the day I've been needing.

And today we won't fight in the morning or afternoon or night, and we will finally fall asleep believing everything is going to be alright.

And maybe today, I'll get some good news, like the cancer is gone or our neighbor decided to mow our lawn.

And today, I'll remember love has been written over my wrongs and now the radio is playing our favorite song:

"Africa" by *Toto*.

And you and I will bless the rains down in Africa and we know, "It's gonna take some time to do the things we never had," but we have time.

And it's about time we have an easy day.

And hopefully tomorrow, too.

GRACE

You were there before my first breath met the light.

When I arrived my blurry eyes grew wide as I kicked and cried, and some days, I'm still kicking and crying as I wonder how and why.

I'm always wondering how and why.

How is this for me?
Why are You for me?

And I'm beginning to believe I should leave the wrestle and rest in the beauty of Your grace, rather than sulk in the misery of my mess and mistakes.

These blurry eyes are beginning to see clearly that there is nothing I can do to save my soul, but You've done what I could not do and You say, "It was all for you."

And it's the endless grace I'll never fully grasp or how You can look at my faults and cracks and still invite me back.

It's the moments of failure I replay in my mind, but You know everything and have somehow forgotten my faults, leaving my wrongs behind.

And You say, "Welcome home," despite who I have been while I'm alone.

And in the end, I will be home because of Your grace and grace alone.

REMAIN

Remain for another day.
Remain with a hope that remains.
Remain to work through the shame.
Remain to fight through the pain.

It's okay to sit with the pain.
To wonder how and why.
To not know what comes next.
Or when to take another step.

And hear me say that's okay.

Our pain needs time.
And our pain needs another by our side.
And our pain is not the end.
But our pain needs time to mend.

And we have time.

And we have each other.

It's okay to sit with the pain
because I know hope remains.

Hope remains.

WAITING. WANDERING. WONDERING.

I am beginning to wonder if You can hear me.
I have whispered and yelled and sat silent and
everything in between.
I have flipped flopped my thumbs, left over right, right over left,
thinking maybe if my hands were folded the right way You would
hear what I have been trying to say.
I have closed my eyes and thought so tight I could feel the veins in
my face become visible.

I have confessed at stop lights, cried out in the middle of sleepless
nights, and have wrestled spite with all my might.

And nothing feels quite right.

Like it says, I have prayed without ceasing and my hands are sore
from releasing.
Or at least they have tried.

If my thoughts are prayers, I cannot stop praying.

I have been wandering around in the waiting
hopefully anticipating, but I am still here wondering.
And waiting.
And hopefully anticipating for Your answer to arrive.

Except for the other day.

We didn't talk or at least I didn't talk to You.
I didn't want to.
It wasn't because I was angry, although I was.
And You knew that.
And it wasn't because I was worried, although I was.
And You knew that, too.

I was scared.
I am scared.
Scared of the potential what if and what now, the constant

questioning of why and how.
Terrified of deconstructing dreams and resetting reality.
Fearful of failing to be faithful through the fire.

And I am tired.

Life was much easier when I was a young boy,
but now that I am older, I am struggling to see through the pain
and uncertainty with hope and joy.

But through it all, somehow, You are working beauty together
with my waiting.

Intertwining peace with patience; time with grace.

Sitting by my side in this unsettled space.

Today, as I wait and wonder, I pray You will keep me from
going under.

May I remain hopeful.
May I remain patient.
May I remain ready.
And may You give me the faith to wait and wonder.

Your way is for the better even if it is taking forever.

SLOW DOWN

LEAN IN

HOLD FAST

KEEP GOING

KEEP GOING

hope forward and go further

Often I find myself writing about hope.

My hands can't help it.

Emily Dickinson says, "Hope is the thing with feathers." And I think that's beautiful, but I had to read the entire poem to understand what she meant.

I get it now.
And she's right.

And I think that's why my hands can't help but write the word hope.

Hope is in me.
It is active.
It is breathing.
It is singing.
It is continuing.
It is calling.

I'm not sure hope can be put into words and perhaps this is why I write about it as often as I do.

Line after line I am attempting to put into words what cannot be put into words.

How do you perfectly describe love?
How do you perfectly put into words joy?
How do you perfectly articulate peace?

This might sound useless, like walking towards a dead end, but for me, writing about hope is a therapeutic reminder of the truth that hope remains and hope is real.

And yet, I've come to believe and see hope is the full assurance of what God will do.

Hope is a peace that continues through the chaos.
Hope is the beauty in the brokenness.
Hope is the certainty that remains in the uncertainty.
Hope is the sun rising and setting and reminding us light is on the way.
Hope is beautiful and heavy and needed and comforting.
Hope reminds me good is here and good is on the way.
Hope invites change, causes growth, and restores joy.

And hope doesn't let the story end, but it keeps our story moving forward.

And that's what I'll keep doing.

I'll keep going.

I'll continue moving forward.

I'll hope forward.

HOPE FORWARD

These two words have been rolling around in my head for the last few weeks.

I'm not sure how they found themselves there, but they haven't left.

They have been a faithful reminder to keep going when it's time to keep going.

Sometimes it's not the right time to move onto what is next.

Sometimes moving forward looks like being still.

Sometimes the right thing to do is to sit and be and rest and wait.

And I'll sit and be and rest and wait with hope.

Without hope it is hard to move forward, but with hope we cannot help but move forward.

I'll hold onto hope as I go.

I'll hope forward as I sit still and take the next step and meet whatever comes my way.

THE LONG WAY HOME

I'm choosing to take the long way home.
I've checked the map and studied story after story.
My finger has run beneath every line, and I've come to realize that even when there are storms in the sky, there are always ways to remain hopeful and dry.

I've got enough soul in my step to keep from sinking and plenty of promises that keep me from panicking.

Along the way, my dirty hands will continue to fold as I pray. Maybe I'll even stumble upon the right words to say.

And today, like it glows at the end of the tunnel, so does the light burn bright inside, reminding me I can take another step.

And I will.

One foot in front of the other with the grace and peace that has led me to be where I am and will take me to where I am going.

And I am going forward and, like I've always found before, I will find that hope has been within me the entire time.

I don't know what is ahead, and I don't need to know.

I've lived through what is behind and somehow, I stand here alive.

I know where I am going.

And this time, I'm choosing to take the long way home.

After all, I'm going home.

HEAVY AND FRAGILE

More and more I've been reminiscing about 2003 and 2004, and as of late I've been wishing it was 2007 or 2008.

Not to change today, but to relive how I became who I am.

I want to retrace my steps, say a little less, try a little harder than my best.
I want to hold tight to the love in my young hands and speak up when I don't understand.
I want to slow down and breathe deep and give you a better memory to keep.
I want to listen close when you tell me life is heavy and fragile instead of waving you off with a half smile.

And maybe it's time to bury the past I'm trying to get back.
And maybe it's time to say goodbye to what was and step into what has beautifully become.

Maybe it's time to take the dirt and sprinkle it over the failures that keep the sun asleep.
Maybe it's time to take the flowers and throw them over the messes I've created and caused.
Maybe it's time to say hallelujah and amen and begin with grace again.
Maybe it's time I come to realize here and now is the only place I was meant to be.

It's all heavy.
It's all fragile.
But all of this is good.

EIGHTH GRADE

The older I grow, the more my memory fades, but there is still a part of me still stuck in 8th grade.

Back when my innocence lived on, we'd stay up late watching *The Adventures of Jimmy Neutron*, these were the days when Stacy's mom had it goin' on and those days are long gone.

And those days, I was slowly beginning to realize that these eyes were growing wide as I journeyed through common 14-year-old lows and highs.

In those days, I had the world in front of me and as far as I could see, life was always going to be young and free.

I had curious questions I would ask without hesitation or fear of rocking the foundation.

I had little worries and big dreams and now I have big worries and little dreams if I can ever stop counting sheep and find the peace to sleep.

But time never stops, and it fails to rewind or be kind, and combined with wondering how and why, I seem confined to feeling behind.

And today I miss not knowing what it's like to be younger than I am.

And today I miss family dinners and recess and not knowing about gray-hair-inducing stress.

And today I miss studying for spelling tests, eating lunch at 10:43 instead of noon, logging on to A.I.M. to say what's up with you, lol, idk, ttyl, be back soon.

I'll never get back to 8th grade and that's okay.

When it comes to time, we always pay a price, and God knows we weren't created to be in middle school twice.

I feel far from the 8th grade boy I once was, but he's still part of me.

And I'm sure 8th grade me would have had question after question about who we came to be.

And all I can say is we aren't done.

If anything, we've just begun.

STILLNESS

My back laid flat as my eyes watched the sky slowly come alive. The sun dipped as the clouds passed, clearing the stage for its shine. And I stared deep into the dark, watching the stars hang still in the space they would light bright. There are only a few things more beautiful than a summer night. I sat still in the silence and remembered I didn't always have to be moving, but I could just be. I could just breathe. I could watch the stars hang from the hands of heaven. I could listen to the sounds of silence under the glow of the moonlight. I could exhale easy and let go of what I've been holding tight. I could be right where I was without wanting or needing to be somewhere or someone else. I could be still. And the stillness continues to call. And one day, I'll be brave enough to accept the invitation to simply be still and breathe free. And all I want is to be still and breathe free. But for some reason, I'm still moving.

NO LONGER INTERNET FRIENDS

According to the internet, we're no longer friends.

You unfollowed me.

And I don't know why.

Maybe someone spoke poorly about me again or gave their perspective on what happened in what they were never involved in.

Or maybe you stopped following me because you got tired of my posts about coffee and poetry and pictures of my life.

Or maybe I said something I shouldn't have said and didn't know I said what I said when I said it.

If so, I'm sorry.

Or maybe you see me differently than I see myself and you're tired of seeing me when you scroll.

But it's cool.

It's cool.

But I am a little confused.

Because at one time, you wanted me in your life and now you don't even want me on your screen.

And now we're no longer Internet friends and I'm not angry, I'm just wondering.

I'm just wondering why.

I'm always just wondering.

But it's cool.

It's cool.

IT'S NICE TO MEET YOU

It's been a while since the last time we've seen each other.

I can only assume that you, like myself, are no longer who you used to be.

Sure, there are shades and shadows of yourself, but like me, you've been turned inside out and upside down.

I have to believe the person I once knew has continued to become and bloom.

This might as well be *nice to meet you* rather than *it's been a while*.

And it has been a while.

Since we last said goodbye, I've gone on and grown.

I've been changed again and again by grace, and I have again and again come face to face with the mistakes that have taken me all over the place.

And those stories you heard about me were of someone I said goodbye to long ago.

Let's not bring him up or into this, for he is no longer with us.

And I know it's not right of me, but I assume the same is true for you as well.

You've become someone new, while somehow holding onto the person I once knew.

Your smile has seen sunrises and miracles.

Your eyes have witnessed life and death.

You've been changed by the seasons and Spirit.

You've come face to face with the past and chose the future.

It's nice to meet you.

You remind me of someone I once knew.

JUST LIKE YESTERDAY

Just like yesterday, the light made its way through the curtains in
our bedroom.
I inhaled deep and exhaled an honest thank you.
The words traveled to God's ears as my eyes opened with freedom.
Another day is here.
So am I.
The dew on the grass was beginning to blindly jump into the sky,
making room for the sunshine to take over its place on the blade.
The world is beginning its morning routine and so was I.
Just like yesterday I put on the coffee.
4 cups.
3 for me.
1 for her.
I need the extra caffeine to keep up with my thoughts.
Our tree in the backyard has taken up a new resident
this past week.
Just like yesterday, she sings a song I'm still trying to learn.
I cannot quite understand her, but I cannot believe it is anything
other than a prayer.
I watch her leave and come back, leave and come back.
She always returns, like she always sings.
Just like yesterday, I wondered what all of this was for.
You know, living.
This endless miracle of breathing and being.
The rollercoaster ride of emotions, the winding road of dreams,
and the uninterrupted movement of becoming.
Just like yesterday, I feel behind.
I got lost when I took a wrong turn by comparing myself to
someone who isn't me.

There is a heaviness and guilt that comes with this way of living.
Some days I think it's true, that I am behind.
But other days, I know it's a lie.
There are many speeds and ways to go forward.
And forward is where I am heading.
Soon it will be tomorrow, but for now it is today and just like
yesterday, I'm again reminding myself that where I am is right
where I need to be.
And it is a beautiful thing to be.
And maybe this is the song the bird sings.

MORE ALIVE

Every day I'm becoming more alive as I leave behind the wrong ways I thought were right.

I'm spending my days walking in grace, and I'm beginning to find peace in this place.

I'm remembering joy,
and holding hope close,
and reminding myself that despite the darkness,

He still rose.

And I am learning to be content with where I am; to accept who I am as I slowly begin to understand I am who He says I am.

And again, I'm on my knees praying for the peace You say is with me.

And it is.

It is with me.

YOUR REMINDER

and this is your reminder
to breathe

and this is your reminder
to let go

and this is your reminder
to rest

and this is your reminder
to trust

and this is your reminder
to keep going

FOR A MOMENT

And for a moment nothing was holding me back or
keeping me down.

I forgot about it all.

I was free.
I was finally free.
I forgot about death.
I forgot about disease.
I forgot about politics.
I forgot about division.

And I forgot about my failures.

I forgot about what I was worrying about moments before.

I, for a moment, was lost in what I can only imagine was grace.

Or peace.
Or love.
Or hope.
Or all the above and then some.

And maybe we are closer to heaven than we think.

We are closer to heaven than we think.

PRODIGAL SON

I was 10 by the time I wanted to be 6, 7, 8, or 9 again.
And if there is one thing I could tell myself back then,
it's what I've been telling myself every now and again: I
am not alone.
And two would be to write until the words rhyme.
And three, four, five,
run until the sun shines,
art is made when you color outside the lines,
and you can believe her when she says, "Everything is going
to be fine."

You can believe her when she says,
"Everything is going to be fine."

I am a lot of things, but one thing I am is becoming.

And I am becoming as I spin and swim through the water and
words splashed and spoken over me.

Becoming as I let the hot questions become coals as they burn,
smoke signals to the sky, my clouded wondering and spinning high.

And I am becoming as I allow myself to sit and be and ask and
turn toward grace and meet you face to face to say, "I don't know."

To say, "I'm sorry."
To say, "I'm learning to let go."
To say, "I've been wrong," but to not be done, because I am a lot
of things, but one thing I am is far from done.
I am far from done,
like the Prodigal son.

Dirty feet to match the past, fear to steal my present, a clouded
mind making beauty blind, quite the contrast from a love that
continues to last.
A light beaming bright with the echo of a Father running to
his Son, speaking and screaming words that keep me from
coming undone.

And I can hear him say, *"Son, welcome home. Welcome back to where you belong."*

And I am a lot of things, but one thing I am not
is my past.
Grace has stretched back to where my memories burn and last.
To misery riddled moments that hold guilt and steal sleep and
make me question You, me, and every little thing.
Grace stretches back to the mistakes made in the wide open
unknown; it stretches back to rock bottom and beyond; it
stretches back with an invitation that will last to begin again and
again and again.

And you can begin again and again and again.

I am a lot of things, but one thing I am is welcomed home.
Where I can be me and rest my weary and wondering eyes, heart,
soul, and feet.

I've returned because of this grace that's been shown and I
don't need to prove I have gone on and grown, and you may
very well always see me for who I used to be, but that boy has
become a man.

Steps changed to follow God's plan.
And I am learning to see me differently.
To see me as He sees me and He sees me differently.
And I am a lot of things, but one thing I am is not alone.

I am not alone.

I am many things.

But I am not alone.

I am welcomed home.

MEET TODAY WITH LOVE

May we meet today with love.

May we meet those who are scared and suffering with grace and peace.

May we reach to those who are vulnerable and fragile with care.

May we see today as the right day to show kindness.

May we step to the lost and hurting with everlasting hope.

May we respond to fear with Your certain love.

May we surrender with the reminder that through it all, You are good.

May we remember You are in control of the unknown.

May we meet today with love.

LIGHT

and it's for you

breaking through

bending and guiding

searching and finding

and somehow it is reminding

me that everything

is going to be okay

THROUGH IT ALL

There is a thread of grace that runs through it all. It's woven through my past and paving the roads ahead. It whispers into the silence and is felt in the chaos. It's written between lines, carved beneath the bark, and burns bright with a single spark. And when I think it isn't there, I take a step back; squint my eyes like I'm staring into the sun and I see. It's there. It's always been there. Grace found us from the start. And I'm beginning to believe it doesn't plan to leave.

...AND BE ORDINARY

The word *ordinary* used to terrify me.

For most of my life I feared this is what my life would become.

Ordinary.

As a teenager, I would lie awake until the early hours of the morning wondering if this life of mine would have lasting impact or if I would be easily forgotten. Selfishly, I worried if I would be a remembered name worthy of a statue or street name or even Wikipedia page.

The acronym Y.O.L.O. (You Only Live Once) (I can't believe I just wrote that in my book) plagued the halls of my high school, attaching to our adolescent minds, acting like lice as it spread across our school's campus. These four letters found their way into our conversations and psyche, changing our view of the world and ourselves. *You Only Live Once* led me to believe I had to become something more than myself, to grab hold of this one life and leave a lasting impression on this earth.

I couldn't shake wanting to stand out; to be *a somebody,* to be remembered.

I wanted to be known and applauded by the world like the greatest basketball player of all time, Michael Jordan or the Fresh Prince, Will Smith or my 8th grade hero: the Fonz, Henry Winkler. In middle school, I went through a big *Happy Days* phase. I'd try to turn on the lights by snapping and casually saying a drawn out "Heyyyy" to girls, just like Fonzie, to see if they'd go out with me. I even tried to convince my mom to get me a leather jacket just like the one he wore in the show, but there is never a good time to wear a leather jacket in Florida.

Beneath my want-to-be-Fonz exterior grew and groaned a lie that I needed to live a life of constant excitement, void of boring and empty of mundane. I thought in order for my life to be significant, to be far from ordinary, it had to be like a movie, full of one liners, first kisses, breakthroughs, and mountain top moments.

Just like Fonzie.

However, by the grace of God, something changed along the way, and my days of dreaming about being remembered as *a somebody* are behind me. No longer do I equate ordinary with *insignificant* or believe I need to have a street named after me to have lived a significant, meaningful life.

I'm not sure when the change took place, but it did.

Maybe it was the silence of a sunset or a Sunday message on mercy.
Maybe it was realizing I am 1 of 7 billion and not just 1
in 7 billion.
Maybe I finally grew still enough to realize this life isn't about me.
Maybe it was realizing beauty, goodness, and joy were already right in front of me.
Maybe it was when I began to believe the words *ordinary* and *insignificant* aren't part of God's vocabulary.

I've come to learn that life is many things, but it is certainly an unfolding; a slow becoming. As I continue to navigate this life, I am beginning to see there is something beautiful about the day by day; the becoming to be.

The steps forward and steps back and steps to the left and right.
The running, the falling, the getting up, and the continuing.
The asking, the wondering, the discovering.

Significance has never been based on who others say you are or what the world may call you, but significance and worth are found in who found you.

And He found me.

Ordinary me.

And now that's who I want to be:

Me.

I only want to be me.

The me He created me to be.

And I want to live an ordinary life.

An extraordinary, ordinary, simple life.

Something small.
Something hidden.
Something less than public.
Something different than I imagined.
Something meaningful.

I want the garden in the backyard and flowers on the front porch.
I want to let my phone's battery drain and see that I am full.
I want to walk down the street and not be recognized.
I want to sit outside at the corner coffee shop with my dog and
have half conversations with familiar strangers as they pass by.
I want to say "I didn't see that," when someone asks me about the
latest scandal or news story or tragedy.
I want to learn how to make something with my hands.
Like a bookcase or a cutting board or an end table.
Or a really good sandwich.
Like, a really, really good sandwich.
I want to do the dishes, make my bed, and mow the lawn.
I want to get on my knees to pray and say amen with confidence.
I want to walk a little slower and live a little deeper.
I want to keep my family and friends close and worry and
fear far away.
I want to be a person of peace and love and rest.
I want to build a campfire and invite you over for an evening.

That's all I want.

An extraordinary, ordinary, simple life.

An extraordinary, ordinary, simple life that God has given me, met
me, and carried me through.

Lately, in the early hours of a new day, I've been saying these three
words to myself:

God is here.

He has met me with the rising sun and welcomed me into a new day. He has placed air in my lungs, thoughts in my mind, feelings in my heart, and hope in my hands. He has called me by name, given me grace, and invited me to live a life of love.

God is here with me.
Ordinary me.

I am not alone.

I am not unknown.

I am not forgotten.

But I am with God.

And God is with me.

Ordinary me.

After all, ordinary isn't meaningless.

Ordinary isn't insignificant.
Ordinary isn't futile.
Ordinary isn't empty.
Ordinary isn't forgotten.

Ordinary is significant.

GO ON

Go on.

Wake up early.
Make the same cup of black coffee.
Put a piece of bread in the toaster.
Toast it until it's golden brown, and not a second earlier.
I know, it's hard to wait.
But wait.
It's almost ready.
Smear Land-O-Lakes butter across the top and don't be stingy.
Life is too short to be stingy.
Don't worry about your phone.
You don't need your phone to eat breakfast.
You don't need your phone to thank God.
You don't need your phone to sip coffee.
You don't need your phone to enjoy the last bite of toast
soaked in butter.
It's a perfect bite.

Say *amen*.

Touch your toes.
Or try.
Or tell them you'll get them in heaven.
Go for a walk.
If you want, the same walk you did yesterday.

As you go, walk a little slower.
Wave to the children.
Pick up the trash.
Wave to the neighbor.
Smile.
Always remember to smile.
Don't be creepy.
But smile.

Look up at the sky.
It's still there.
It was there yesterday, too.
Did you see it?
God made the sky.
God made the clouds.
God made the sun.
God made the wind.
God made the birds.
You can wave to them, too.
You can feed them, too.

Do you see the trees?
You don't need your phone to look at the trees.
They're changing and changing and changing.
Just like you.
Becoming season after season.
Growing through the storms; swaying in the sunlight.
Look at the trees and remember how they came to be.
Like your faith, it all started with a little seed.
And how beautiful it is to believe.
You don't need your phone to believe.

Do the day.
As you go, don't forget the grace that got you here.
Remember mercy.
Remember love.
Remember that phone call you have at 3:00 PM.
You need your phone for that phone call.
Remember that thing you need to do, but remember that the thing
you need to do will not change your worth.
Remember to take the chicken out of the freezer so it can thaw.
You cannot have chicken tacos for dinner with frozen chicken.

Remember to drink water.
Remember hope.
Remember faithfulness.

Remember her birthday is coming up.
There is always something and someone to celebrate.
You are also someone worth celebrating.
But this life isn't about you.
I know, it can be confusing.
Life is confusing.
But it's also worth celebrating.
Remember peace.
Remember self-control.
Remember to call.

Tell them you love them.
Tell them you miss them.

Remember kindness.
Remember goodness.
Mow the lawn.
Pull the weeds.
Plant the seeds.
Remember joy.
Remember patience.
Look up at the sky.
It's still there.
Remember the trees.
Remember all of this is worth staying for.

And at night, step outside one last time.
Watch the sun fall into the silence of the horizon.
A daily reminder we were made to rest and rise and repeat.
Rest and rise and repeat.
Feel the light of the setting sun dance on your skin.

You're alive.
You're covered in grace.
You're known.
You're loved.

I hate when people remind me I am known and loved.

You're known.
You're loved.

The stars shine above you; for you.
You're seen.
You're significant.

From your head to the toes you cannot touch.
From your insides where the coffee mixes with golden brown toast
to your outside where the light hugs your skin like an old friend
saying hello.
From your waking to your sleeping.
From your wondering to your realizing.
From your season to season.
From your first breath to your last.
You're significant.
And you don't need your phone to be significant.

Go on.

ACKNOWLEDGMENTS

Thank you to James Saleska, Tim Bauer, Andrew Milam, and Sarah Olson for giving your time and gifts to this book.

Huge thanks to my Patrons for supporting my work and dreams as a writer and poet.

I am forever grateful for you. Thank you for sharing my work around, buying copies for your friends and family, and for not calling me terrible names on the internet or to my face. Lord knows my sensitive heart would not handle it well.

To my family and friends and those friends who are family. Thank you for believing in this book and for reminding me of my purpose and identity in Christ.

Thanks be to God for dogs, grace, coffee, and sunshine. All have played an important role in the writing of this book.

Sarah, I love you. Let's go get coffee and take Pancake on a big walk.

ABOUT THE AUTHOR

Tanner Olson is an author, poet, and speaker living in Nashville, TN with his wife Sarah and their dog, Pancake.

Tanner started writing in 2013 and began sharing his work under the name Written to Speak. The mission of Tanner's writing is to spread hope and announce love through written and spoken word poetry.

He is the author of *I'm All Over the Place: A Book of Poems, Prayers, and Wonderings* and *As You Go: Words for the Unknown*.

From classrooms to churches to organizations to coffee shops, Tanner has traveled across the country performing poetry, delivering messages of hope, and sharing stories.

To bring Tanner to your next event, visit writtentospeak.com.

Facebook: facebook.com/writtentospeak
Instagram: @writtentospeak
Twitter: @tannerJolson
Support: patreon.com/writtentospeak

Made in United States
North Haven, CT
30 October 2023

43383456R00072